SPIN
A SOFT
BLACK
SONG

REVISED EDITION

SQUARE
FISH

Farrar Straus Giroux • New York

For Wendy, Bruno, V.W., Holly, and Rocky,
who sit in silent castles
N. G.

SQUARE
FISH

An Imprint of Macmillan

Library of Congress Cataloging-in-Publication Data
Giovanni, Nikki.
Spin a soft Black song : poems for children / by Nikki Giovanni ; illustrated by George Martins.
ISBN 978-0-374-46469-1
1. African American children—Juvenile poetry. 2. Children's poetry, American.
[1. African Americans—Poetry. 2. American poetry—African American authors.]
I. Martins, George, ill. II. Title.
PS3557.I55 S68 1985   811'.54'0809282   84-19287

Originally published in the United States by Farrar Straus Giroux
Revised edition: 1985
First Square Fish Edition: September 2012
Square Fish logo designed by Filomena Tuosto
mackids.com

29 30

LEXILE: NP

The Tunnels of Rumpelstiltskin

Rumpelstiltskin was probably the most misunderstood man of his time . . . His trusting nature was violated by witches . . . who sold his secret . . . and profaned his profession . . . to curry the favor of princes . . . Hurt and frustrated . . . he danced a moon dance . . . boring his imprudence and bewilderment into the center . . . of his heart and our earth . . . burying his loom in tunnels unknown.

In Hamlin . . . finding himself cheated and deceived . . . a more astute man wove magic around music . . . spun a soft Black song . . . to destroy the vermin . . . and empower the children . . . He triumphantly opened mountains in the sky . . . planting his flute as a masthead for doves . . . waltzing his Hansels and Gretels to dreams.

The waltz is a graceful dance . . . originally performed by swans . . . on a quiet lake . . . for the sheer joy . . . that beauty brings.

Flamingos dance . . . a merry waltz . . . upon blue waters . . . caressing white sands . . . celebrating day's end . . . welcoming the night.

City streets at night . . . like Dr. Jekyll and Mr. Hyde . . . can change from friendly play and laughter places . . . to scary dark and vacant holes . . . City streets do not dance a waltz . . . They wait . . . pacing panthers encircling prey . . . for release.

I mine the tunnels of Rumpelstiltskin . . . I seek the secret of his Black loom . . . not for the pedestrian purpose of spinning flax into gold . . . or for the obsequience of helping peasant girls be acceptable concubines to ineffectual princes . . . The magic I forge frustration and deceit to rediscover will uncover the desire of Prometheus to bring fire from the sky . . . the need of Noah to construct an ark to the future . . . the challenge to Pandora to disarm that which she allowed to escape from her trunk.

I seek the courage of a boy . . . who could go into the Temple to assail the knowledge of the Elders . . . The confidence of a man . . . to pronounce the earth a satellite of the sun . . . The curiosity of a woman . . . to see not only those aspects unseen but those unseeable.

I share the desire to plant a masthead for doves . . . to spin a soft Black song . . . to waltz with the children . . . to the mountains of our dreams.

Nikki Giovanni
Herrington Lake, 1984

Spin a Soft Black Song

dance poem

come nataki dance with me
bring your pablum dance with me
pull your plait and whorl around
come nataki dance with me

won't you tony dance with me
stop your crying dance with me
feel the rhythm of my arms
don't let's cry now dance with me

tommy stop your tearing up
don't you hear the music
don't you feel the happy beat
don't bite tony dance with me
mommy needs a partner

here comes karma she will dance
pirouette and bugaloo
short pink dress and dancing shoes
karma wants to dance with me
don't you karma don't you

all you children gather round
we will dance and we will whorl
we will dance to our own song
we must spin to our own world
we must spin a soft Black song
all you children gather round
we will dance together

poem for ntombe iayo
(at five weeks of age)

who them people think
they are putting
me down here
on this floor

i'll just lay
here stretching
my arms and maybe i'll kick
my legs a li'l bit

why i betcha i'll just get up
from here and walk
soons i get big

let's take a nap

almost every day
after my lunch
after my milk
after i go to the potty
and teddy and piggy, my green turtles,
have been fed
and i can't think of anything to do quick enough
mommy says "come on chocolate drop"
'cause she thinks i don't remember what she wants
"let's take a nap"
just 'cause i'm a little feller don't mean i'm dumb!
then she takes off my shoes and pants and hops me
into her big bed
and i have to:
    climb on her chest
    be tossed in the air
    get tickled under my chin
    hear this little piggy three times
    and get the bottom of my feet kissed
        at least twice
before i put her
to sleep

for deena

deena-gina
child
fat child
pretty child
child of
Black child
happy child
next door neighbor
child
of my child
hood

one of the problems of play

every time
before i go out
my mother says
do you have to go
and i say "no" and i go
out but then
i play hard and have to
go and i don't like to
go in when i'm out
so i go out
side when i'm out

mommies

MOMMIES
  make you brush your teeth
  and put your old clothes on
  and clean the room
  and call you from the playground
  and fuss at daddies and uncles
  and tuck you in at night
  and kiss you

daddies

DADDIES
   throw you in the air
   let you blow out matches
   tell you GET OUT THERE AND FIGHT AND
      DON'T COME BACK TILL YOU WIN
   laugh till the house shakes
   teach you how to walk and wear a hat
   and pee

shopping

i know it's time
we've watched Sesame Street ten times
and every ten times is time
i'd better pretend i don't care one way
or the other
   "come on sugar dumpling mommy has to go
   to the store"
i'd better not be too easy
   "Abxyn qpotz?"
let her coax me
   "come on apple cake put your coat on"
maybe i'll push her a little
   "Qpy Skt?"
she's getting that exasperated look
   "i'm gonna leave you terrance if you don't
   come on"
god! i hope she lets me ride on top again i hope
she's forgotten the last time and doesn't make me
    take the walker
i'd better stand tall
   "Sptp Q?"
   "oh you want to walk do you"
   "Ab X?"

"well young man the last time i took you
    to the grocery store . . ."
curses "abk soi cacaca!" foiled again!

mommies do

in summer
mommy goes to work and locks
me in
and i peep outside through the iron
gate at the children playing
ball and rope and scaley and break
bottles and run and jump
and laugh
and i ask mommy why can't i
go out and mommy says because
she loves me

trips

eeeveryyee time
when i take my bath
and comb my hair (i mean
mommy brushes it till i almost cry)
and put on my clean clothes
and they all say MY
HOW NICE YOU LOOK
and i smile and say
"thank you mommy cleaned
me up"
then i sit down and mommy says
GET UP FROM THERE YOU GONNA BE DIRTY
'FORE I HAVE A CHANCE TO GET DRESSED
    MYSELF
and i want to tell her if you was
my size the dirt would catch
you up faster too

fear

early evening fear
comes i turn
on the television for company
and see
the news

dreams

i get up at seven o'clock
every morning and dress
and run downstairs

i am usually the first
on my block to watch
the traffic come and go
        come and goooooo
        come and go
to watch the traffic come
and gooooooooooo
and i dream i was
goooooooo toooooooo

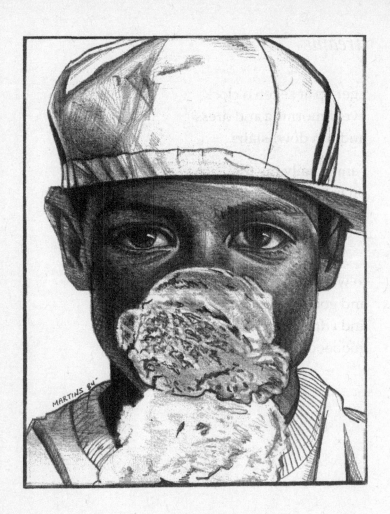

james shell's snowball stand

snowballs are fun
when the streets are covered
with white liquid
but they mean much more to me
when james puts raspberry and cherry
on them in july

some things are funny like that

i went to the school
yard to play and be happy
and the man scowled down
and asked WHAT IS MY AFFILIATION
and i said i wasn't sick
at all and only had one cold once
last year
then he said WHERE IS YOUR BUTTON
and i said my zipper almost always
works but sometimes i forget but i looked
and saw it was all the way
up
and he said LITTLE BOY THIS PLAY
GROUND IS FOR BLACK CHILDREN
and i said i was Black right
on and he said HOW
DID I KNOW and i said mister
i'm gonna just go on
home now and i waved at him
good-bye

two friends

lydia and shirley have
two pierced ears and
two bare ones
five pigtails
two pairs of sneakers
two berets
two smiles
one necklace
one bracelet
lots of stripes and
one good friendship

george

the Jackson Five beamed
STOP to george who
sitting on the stoop and drawing the faces
said the love i save
is wasted

yvonne

yvonne
stood there unsmiling
with collard greens
and sensible shoes
on her way
to becoming a good
Black woman

barbara poems

are round and soft
with explosives inside

but don't let that
scare you

shirley and her son

some people own lots of land
some live in apartment houses
some people have big fine cars
some ride the subways
some people travel all over
some never leave harlem
some people think they own the world
and some people like shirley
don't care if they do 'cause
she thinks the whole of the universe is wrapped
up in her little tom-tom

poem for rodney

people always ask what
am i going to be
when i grow
up and i always
just think
i'd like to grow
up

poem for debbie

who is tall and bold
with sneakers to make
her run faster to
or from
the world

the boy in the barber shop

philip stands
in the doorway
frowning
i want to smile and say come
inside

chester's wisdom

chester said fishing
is a good thing
to do even
if you don't catch
anything and even if
you do then
you can cook
or not and i thought
uh-huh that's something
to know

parents never understand

well i can't 'cause
yesterday when mommy had
this important visitor she said
run along joey and let mommy talk
and i ran along upstairs to see
bobby and eddie and we were playing
and forgot and i had to come down
stairs and get dry clothes and mommy said how
could an eight year old boy wet his pants
and i looked at the visitor and smiled a really nice
smile and said i guess in america anything
can happen
so mommy said i have to
stay in today

springtime

in springtime the violets
grow in the sidewalk cracks
and the ants play furiously
at my gym-shoed toes
carrying off a half-eaten peanut
butter sandwich i had at lunch
and sometimes i crumble
my extra graham crackers
and on the rainy days i take off
my yellow space hat and splash
all the puddles on Pendry Street and not one
cold can catch me

the drum

daddy says the world is
a drum tight and hard
and i told him
i'm gonna beat
out my own rhythm

ten years old

i paid my 30¢ and rode by the bus
window all the way down

i felt a little funny with no hair
on my head
but my knees were shiny 'cause
aunty mai belle cleaned me up
and i got off on time and walked
past the lions and the guard straight
up to the desk and said
   "dr. doolittle steroscope please"
and this really old woman said
   "Do You Have A Library Card?"
and i said
   "i live here up the street"
and she said
   "Do You Have a LIBRARY Card?"
and i said
   "this is the only place i can use the steroscope
     for
   dr. dooolittle miss washington brought us here
     this spring
   to see it"

and another lady said
  "GIVE THE BOY WHAT HE WANT. HE
      WANT TO LEAD THE RACE"
and i said
  "no ma'am i want to see dr. dooolittle"
and she said "same thang son same thang"

basketball

when spanky goes
to the playground all the big boys say
   hey big time—what's happenin'
'cause his big brother plays basketball for their
      high school
and he gives them the power sign and says
   you got it
but when i go and say
   what's the word
they just say
   your nose is running junior

one day i'll be seven feet tall
even if i never get a big brother
and i'll stuff that sweaty ball down
their laughing throats

education

mama got out and fussed
real good 'bout the schools
'cause i'm in the eighth
grade and she wants me to continue
but she says she needs to be
sure i don't become
just another high
school student

sleep

it was dark but when i blinked
twice i could see all the way deep
into the forest
and the lion came at me
and i really took care of him (pooped him twice
in the nose)
then a big rhinoceros with purple dots
and bright pink eyes
and i flung him over my head and threw
him into his mother's lap (where he belongs
since i'm so badddd)
then this striped horse neighed
up on his hind feet
but i jumped high and bit his ear
and he ran away crying
also the big bird whose wings blotched
out the moonlight swooped down
on me and i tickled his feet
just before the talons sunk in
and he laughed and laughed and slapped me
on the back and went home

so it's easy to see when the rat climbed
into my bed how tired
i was and why i called
   mooooooooommmmmmmmmmiiiiiiiiieeeeeeeeeeee

mrs. martha jean black

they call mrs. black the mother
of the church and most sundays she says
"gregory do you know your 'scription?"
and i say "blessed are the meek"
and she gives me a nickel and says
"mind yo mama"
and i say "yes ma'am" and go to the store
and have candy
i like mrs. black

mattie lou at twelve

they always said "what a pretty little girl you are"
and she would smile

they always said "how nice of you to help
your mother with your brothers and sisters"
and she would smile and think

they said "what lovely pigtails you have
and you plaited them all by yourself!"
and she would say "thank you"

and they always said "all those B's
what a good student you are"
and she would smile and say thank you

they said "you will make a fine woman some
    day"
and she would smile and go her way

because she knew

stars

in science today we learned
that stars are a mass of gases that burned
out a long time ago only we don't know
that because we still see the glow

and i remembered my big brother donny
said he burned out a long time ago and i asked
him did that make him
a star

a heavy rap

i can run faster than any gazelle
last time i had a race i left him
on the inside corner of the indy 500
i can outswim any ole fish
gave a dolphin a half-hour start
and still beat him across the ocean
i mean i'm so bad i gave a falcon
a half-mile lead and beat him to the top
of the mountain
i roared so loud the lion hung his head
in shame and his wife came and asked me to
        please
leave that part of the jungle as her husband's
        feelings
were so hurt by my together thing
i had a jumping contest with a kangaroo and
jumped clear outa australia and passed the
        astronauts
on their way back down
i can rap so hard Rap Brown hates to be
in the same town with me
and i'm only ten
this year coming

if

if he could climb a tree
he'd be Matthew Henson exploring
the north pole surveying all of the world
watching the sun and the moon stand still
in awe and wonder of each other

if he could descend into a cave he might
be the man in Harriet Tubman's life
giving her support and direction
on her journeys south

if he lived in a forest he'd learn
to know the berries and how to whittle
a sapling into a switch and which animals
were friendly and which weren't

if he lived in a civilized world
he'd learn that all is love

By Nikki Giovanni

POETRY

Those Who Ride the Night Winds
Cotton Candy on a Rainy Day
The Women and the Men
My House
Re: Creation
Black Feeling, Black Talk/Black Judgment

POETRY FOR CHILDREN

Vacation Time
Ego Tripping and Other Poems for Young Readers
Spin a Soft Black Song

ESSAYS AND DIALOGUES

A Poetic Equation: Conversations Between
Margaret Walker and Nikki Giovanni

A Dialogue: James Baldwin and Nikki Giovanni

Gemini: An Autobiographical Statement on
My First Twenty-five Years